Gerald Madsen

A New Home

Young Adults and Transisional Housing

Anchor Compact

Madsen, Gerald: A New Home: Young Adults and Transisional Housing.
Hamburg, Anchor Academic Publishing 2014
Original title of the thesis: «buchtitel»

Buch·ISBN: 978·395489·197·9
PDF·eBook·ISBN: 978·3·95489·697·4
Druck/Herstellung: Anchor Academic Publishing, Hamburg, 2014

Bibliografische Information der Deutschen Nationalbibliothek:
Die Deutsche Nationalbibliothek verzeichnet diese Publikation in der Deutschen
Nationalbibliografie; detaillierte bibliografische Daten sind im Internet über
http://dnb.d·nb.de abrufbar

Bibliographical Information of the German National Library:
The German National Library lists this publication in the German National Bibliography.
Detailed bibliographic data can be found at: http://dnb.d·nb.de

© Anchor Academic Publishing, ein Imprint der Diplomica® Verlag GmbH
http://www.diplom.de, Hamburg 2014
Printed in Germany

Table of contens

Abstract

Homeless young adults represent a failure of the U.S. social services system to prevent new generations of homeless people. However, several organizations are working in concert with communities and governments to combat this problem through transitional housing programs that target young adults ages 18 to 24. Many of these programs mirror the new urban development trend of mixed-income housing, and place transitional houses inside stable neighborhoods that are either affluent or mixed-income themselves. While these programs represent monumental commitments in terms of resources, they also represent hope for many young adults. The sense of community these young-adult residents feel toward their neighborhoods and programs have lasting effects on the residents' abilities to find normalcy inside the American culture through access to education, safety, and employment. This study examines the YMCA Young Adult Services Program (serving the greater Seattle area) for transitional housing, exploring how the program works and what is residents' psychological sense of community.

Keywords: transitional housing, young adults, homelessness, mixed income housing, psychological sense of community

1   Introduction

Urban development and community planning date back to the design of Miletus and Alexandria by the Greek Hippodamus around 407 BC (Jackson, 1985). From that time onward, planning and developing of urban environments evolved into a standard process for city and community leaders. In modern times, the process revitalizes slums, creates new neighborhoods, and manages residents. Contemporarily, urban development and community planning are tools that unite peoples across socio-economic statuses and result in the gentrification of low-income residents (Chaskin & Joseph, 2012; Jones, 1990). In the United States, Community Development Corporations (CDC), religious groups, and social groups use these tools to support impoverished and marginalized populations (Chaskin & Karlström, 2012; Martin, 2011). Dating back to Jane Addams and the Settlement House movement in the 1800s (Martin, 2011; Murrin et al., 2008; Naveh, 1992) and evolving into a plethora of development organizations, ranging from John Perkins' Christian-based[1] development programs (Perkins, 1982) to the U.S. government's HOPE VI program (Kang 2010; Katz, Liebow, & O'Malley, 2006), there is a clear tradition in the United States of aiding and working with the poor.

Current U.S. housing policies—both public and private—use several strategies to address poverty and aid, from reconstructing urban slums to restructuring governmental programs that address housing (Schill, 1999) to creation of mixed-income neighborhoods built and managed by the private sector and neighborhood residents. Through housing agencies, CDCs, and advocacy groups, low-income neighborhoods are restructured to support the success of residents, without gentrifying them so poor people become displaced (Chaskin & Joseph, 2012; Chaskin & Joseph 2011; Galster & Zobel, 1998; Stoutland, 1999; Wier, 1999). As these programs progress, it is apparent that an entire population is being left behind, the homeless. Modern housing programs target those already housed; these programs elevate low-income people and families through development of mixed-income housing, appropriate social capital, and creation of community. Although alleviation of poverty is essential to the housing policy mission, alleviation of homelessness—with the exception of housing policy in New York City—is not (Schill, 1999).

Housing programs are often designed to help or elevate the housed, regardless of socio-economic status,[2] leaving the homeless an underserved population in terms of safe, affordable, and equitable housing. Housing problems are compounded further by the fact that many communities perceive homeless people negatively (Vissing, 1996). It is imperative that housing policy consider homeless people because of the influences community development and urban planning have on homeless populations. It is important to understand urban planning, community development, and the impacts these tools have not only on low-income populations, but also on the community as a whole, including those both housed and homeless.

Due to similarities between stigmas and stereotypes higher socio-economic classes hold toward homeless and low-income people, this understanding begins by examining studies of new, mixed-income developments. These developments attempt to create stable and sustainable communities, the results of which are communities that include a cross-section of cultures, beliefs, and peoples across socio-economic statuses. To create these communities, it is important to understand the effectiveness of the programs and the social interactions observable in the neighborhoods. As Karlan and Appel (2011) discuss, it is important for development work to submit to empirical study. In the context of mixed-income housing, particularly in and near Chicago, these studies have been and are being conducted to better understand the effects of social change in relation to housing environments. That understanding can then be used as a foundation for examining how homeless populations behave in mixed-income settings.

Homeless populations form a meta-society that is just as diverse and rich in culture, heritage, and beliefs as others are. While examining how planning and development influence low-income neighborhoods, separate community identities and affiliated cultural citizenships that exist between low-income and homeless populations must be considered; it is imperative that researchers examine the identities and citizenships of the various subgroups inside urban homeless populations. From war veterans to recently homeless families, from children to the elderly, each group deserves a distinct solution that empowers each member.

1.1. Liberation Theology and Empowerment

Using the ideal of group empowerment, the tenets of liberation theology come into play. As Groody (2009) explains, liberation theology is a Catholic tool for not only applying theory, but also creating an effective response that is meaningful to an environment and people. It works by addressing the reality of the situation, then reflecting on scripture, cultural requirements, and the views of the people. Finally, a practitioner of liberation theology formulates a response to the environment that empowers the people in need; the idea is not only to empower homeless populations, but also to reorganize the social system, making members the primary agents of their own restorations (Boff, 1997).

Liberation theology goes deeper still. Since the theological tenets are based both culturally and socially, it demands that each group in the process seeks an understanding of the other's culture and humanity. It requires that judgments based on race, religion, etc. be stilled, granting each group a fresh and unique path toward empowerment. Using Groody's methodology, one must first understand a specific subpopulation, be it couch-surfing teens, mentally ill people, young families, etc. However, understanding does not end with the population's demographics; it includes culture and history too. One must reflect on that understanding, from both the larger viewpoint of spirituality and/or secular study and the micro view of the population. Next one must move beyond power dynamics that favor the aid worker, instead aiding in the creation of programs that places homeless people as empowering agents. Finally, one must understand that not everyone is ready or willing to become empowered, and have the time, patience, and will to wait for stragglers to appear.

Using liberation theology and a need to focus on a single population, this paper focuses on previously homeless young adults (PHYA) in the greater Seattle area. The subpopulation under study is the one closest to those currently residing in mixed-income housing: previously homeless young adults in transitional housing in the greater Seattle area. Similarities between residents in mixed-income neighborhoods and PHYAs include access to social programs designed to elevate participants and pressures on young adults to conform to neighborhood standards. The purpose of this study is to determine whether PHYAs acclimate to their housing and neighborhoods, and attempt to determine a sense of community. Although YouthCare is mentioned frequently in this study, participants were residents, staff members, and resident managers of the YMCA's Young Adult Services (YAS) transitional housing program for the greater Seattle area. Stated earlier, the two groups share multiple similarities; primary among them is inclusion of multiple socio-economic groups in one neighborhood. This study draws from extant research examining mixed-income housing to corroborate and further findings, and generalizable across disparate areas, primarily Seattle and Chicago.

The format of this paper was designed to explain common terms and methods that appear in extant research and this study. It presents findings on mixed-income housing, including an analysis of psychological sense of community. The structure of the YMCA's Young Adult Services program is discussed, and a narrative of one resident's journey from homelessness to housing is presented. Finally, findings and conclusions drawn from interviews and surveys presented to residents, managers, and direct service staff members at the YMCA are discussed, focusing especially on residents' senses of community and belonging in relation to their houses and neighborhoods.

1.2   Limitations

The methodology used in this study was designed to contribute to the growing knowledge of previously homeless young adults in the greater Seattle area. This was achieved partially through application of methods used in other areas of sociological and anthropological research concerning poverty, housing, and cultural identity. The intent was to gauge feelings of community in the target population toward their neighborhoods and the YMCA YAS program. Limitations of this study center on the short time in which data were gathered. Of 48 persons who can be housed in the Y's transitional housing programs, seven were reached by survey (15%) and five were available for interviews. This limits conclusions drawn concerning all youths who participate in the program, and to four of seven houses from which Residents participated. Views of other neighborhood residents were not obtained. Data concerning incomes, racial/ethnic distributions, occupations, and education for this group were obtained from a third party. Therefore, the exact statuses of the neighborhoods were left to some interpretation on behalf of the researcher. Results of this study were limited to the people interviewed and surveyed. Although a significant portion of the YMCA Transitional Housing program residents were surveyed, the surveys may not reflect aggregate views of the population.

2   Methods

Much of the development of this study drew from extant research conducted in Chicago by researchers examining the phenomenon of mixed-income housing developments, but was not limited to those studies. Research on cultural inclusion and identity covering Seattle's International district, discussions on sense of community, and many other works served as foundational works for this study. Much of this study's vocabulary, processes, and surveys were based on the works of others, retooled for use with PHYAs in Seattle. This section reports on those items, starting with vocabulary, an explanation of survey and interview processes, and the importance of using U.S. Census Bureau tract data for population comparisons.

2.1.Vocabulary

When examining a social phenomenon, it is important to define the parameters and vocabulary to be used. Slight nuances in meaning can not only change the explanation of outcomes, but also alter understandings of the events observed and explained.

Previously Homeless Young Adults and Homelessness. In this paper, "previously homeless young adults" (PHYA) refers to people 18 to 24 years old who were homeless prior to entering a transitional housing program. PHYAs are also addressed as "client residents", indicating their status in a transitional housing program. Homeless people include all people who lack permanent housing, including people who couch-surf from friend to friend, people who due to their gender, sexuality, or the abusive nature of their household are at risk of being homeless, and throw-away people who were denied access to their homes by family members.

In this population, YouthCare (*Why are youth homeless?*, n.d.) suggests 74% of their encountered population have been abused physically at home, and 39% were abused sexually. Forty percent of encountered persons self-identify as lesbian, gay, bisexual, transgender, or questioning (LGBTQ), and many in this group were kicked out of their homes for being LGBTQ. Finally, there are the people who have had a bad life. A death in the family, the loss of a job (either through a parent or self), or loss of home through manmade or natural disaster can deposit a person on the streets.

The scope of the PHYA population needs to be considered. In King County, the population is estimated at 302 young adults (*Count us in*, 2013). This number represents 39% of the 776 participants (678 were aged 18 to 25) surveyed in the *Count Us In* (*Count us in*, 2013) census of homeless and unstably housed young people. Although this number represents a small percentage of King County's 1.9 million residents (Felt, 2011), it is only a snapshot of those people present or reachable on the day the survey was administered.

Psychological Sense of Community. A definition of psychological sense of community (PSOC) was taken from Brodsky, O'Campo, and Aronson (1999), who examine the individual and community factors that contribute to a sense of community in low-income, intercity neighborhood. The researchers suggest that such communities have positive environments, something not often perceived to exist by outsiders in lower-class neighborhoods. PSOC works in concert with social capital, and represents the links among individuals, families and organizations. PSOC goes beyond identifying mere support structures, and represents positive, negative, and indifferent outlook on one's own community. PSOC is a subjective measure, capturing a respondent's views of community at the time of a survey or interview. For this study, PSOC was gauged through respondents' answers to a survey (Appendix I) and interview questions concerning use of neighborhood facilities, how they felt about their neighbors, their sense of safety inside the neighborhood, and their willingness to participate in community events.

Transitional Housing. In the YouthCare program, short-term housing is called transitional housing or independent living. The first stabilizes residents, providing a safe environment for them. The independent living program is a transition from stabilization to normalcy in mainstream society. Within these programs, YouthCare provides housing specifically designed for LGBTQ residents. YMCA Young Adults Services (YMCA-YAS) offers a similar program, though with a single stage called short-term housing, which includes 48 units located throughout the greater Seattle area. Similar to YouthCare, the YMCA-YAS program is designed to aid client residents transition from homelessness to normalcy.

The programs share similar term limits, ranging from 15 to 24 months, and require residents to be employed, volunteering, or enrolled in school during their stay. The primary difference between the programs comes in the form of rent. In YouthCare programs, rent is a function of income; a standard percentage is used to calculate each resident's rent. At the conclusion of the program, the money is returned to the client. For YMCA-YAS, rent does not vary with income; it is a set rate, and it is not held and returned to the resident when exiting the program.

Mixed-Income Housing. Mixed-income housing is any neighborhood where more than one socio-economic level is present regularly. For developments currently under construction in Chicago, this is a planned environment, representing a predetermined number of low-income renters, middle and working-class renters and owners, and occasionally upper-middle-class owners. When applied to PHYAs, it refers to housing that may appear in affluent neighborhoods. For example, YouthCare's Iisi house is for LGBT residents, and is situated near Ravenna Park—a neighborhood traditionally populated by graduate students and professors from the University of Washington (Wilma, 2001). YMCA-YAS has similar locations for transitional housing (A. Fox, personal communication, January 17, 2013).

Resilience. Resilience means an ability of a person or thing to resist another (Resistance, 2013). Chaskin (2008) uses a new definition of the word. Examining the concept of community, Chaskin redefines resilience to represent a person or community's ability to adapt to adverse conditions by drawing on local resources to negate negative outcomes. For example, a person able to draw on social networks to cope with homelessness by locating semi-permanent or permanent shelters shows higher resilience than a person who accepts homelessness. In a community aspect, it represents a community's ability to deal with disasters or changing economic times or demographics positively. Resilience demonstrates a person's or community's fundamental adaptation system (Chaskin, 2008).

Cultural Citizenship and Community Identity. Cultural citizenship takes on Ong's definition (as cited in Kang, 2010, pp. 4-5), but an adaptation was made for this study. Instead of referring to minority ethnic/majority ethnic society as Ong intended, it describes the bipolar relationship between high (rich) and low (poor) socio-economic statuses. Here low socio-economic status supplants the minority ethnic group. This altered definition describes a dialectic process that refuses the condition of privilege to either the regulating power of the rich or the ability of the poor to choose their path freely without acknowledging society's restraints. Under this definition, the rich are denied the ability to dictate the course of the poor. The poor, in turn, are required to acknowledge they work inside a constraining

14

system that includes civil society, social services, and in the context of a mixed-income setting, other socio-economic statuses.

Community identity becomes both a byproduct of cultural citizenship and a method of facilitating that citizenship; it becomes the mutual society to which all members subscribe. Community has been traditionally a product of spatial definitions (Chaskin & Joseph, 2009), but Sampson's (1999) argument that restraining the concept of community physically debilitates the sense of community is acknowledged. Although studies mentioned here include communities that are limited spatially, people living in these areas have community connections such as family, church, and employment that exist outside of this space. The extensions of community beyond spatial limitations of a neighborhood become the social networks that comprise social capital.

Social Capital. Claridge (2012) argues there are several definitions of social capital. Regardless of the author, most definitions carry the element of relationships and communities that link two or more people, definitions that accord with George Herbert Mead's classic social theory (Edles & Appelrouth, 2010) in which the self-interacts with the other (society) as a method of cultural exchange and creation of identity. Here, social capital is represented as social networks of which each person is a part, without taking the position of being positive or negative. The social relationships between people, and connections between positions, represent the networks (Sampson, 1999), and wealth of capital is measured by the ability of each person to wield their network. This means that a homeless person possesses social capital, and a PHYA wielded the wealth represented through that capital to acquire housing. Although this measure removes the ability of one group to strip the ideal of social capital from another, it does acknowledge the limitations this form of capital represents. These limitations are present in cultural citizenship and represented by the constraining systems that bind each socio-economic class.

Maximum Population. Maximum population refers to the maximum number of residents that can participate in the program. Due to the transitional nature of these housing programs, a single head count solely represents the day the count was made, and cannot represent the program as a whole since applicants are continually in the process of filling empty slots.

To ascertain the sense of community felt by residents in the YMCA-YAS Transitional housing program, surveys and interviews were conducted with staff members and residents. The interviews were conducted in person by phone and email. Resident managers distributed and collected surveys. In all cases in which data were collected from a resident, personal identifying information was kept confidential, and pseudonyms were assigned to respondents to maintain organic flow in the paper.

Interviews were conducted in three populations: YMCA-YAS resource specialists (case managers), YMCA resident managers (who live on-site), and the residents themselves. Interviews conducted with Y resource specialists were unstructured and used open-ended questions. These interviews were conducted in person at the YMCA-YAS main office site in the Rainer Valley district of Seattle. Interviews with resident managers were structured, used a standard set of questions (Appendix II), and were conducted by email or phone. Residents were the only participants who completed both group interviews and surveys (Appendix I). Answers to the survey were coded and used to guide group interviews with residents. Residents who participated in the group interviews received a participation incentive of US$20. The only exception to the group interview process was Subject 1 or Sue, who was part of an individual, unstructured interview. Once interviews were completed, they were coded so Brodsky et al.'s (1999) concept of psychological sense of community could be applied.

2.2   ZIP Codes, Census Tracts & Housing Location

Neighborhoods were broken down first by U.S. Postal Service ZIP Codes and then further by U.S. Census tracts, and examined based on age, race/ethnicity, and income. They were examined to determine whether the tract, including the YMCA-YAS shared home, counted as mixed income. A comparative analysis was conducted to judge whether integration of the PHYAs into the neighborhood was successful.

Census tracts are subsets of ZIP Codes that represent spatial data on race and population, but lack income data that discern socio-economic class inside each tract. Zooming out to the level of ZIP Codes, overall income data—though important for the larger neighborhood—are too general for specific tracts. However, data from ZIP Codes are used to ascertain the larger neighborhood's status.

U.S. Postal ZIP Codes. For the 2010 census, the U.S. Census Bureau did not collect income data at levels lower than ZIP Codes. Therefore, income and demographic data are represented at the ZIP code level to evaluate the population surrounding the YMCA-YAS shared home to determine whether the area is mixed-income in relation to the house. That last part is most important since population density could dilute socio-economic statuses of house residents and a neighborhood that is comprised of a single socio-economic status.

U.S. Census Bureau Tracts. Once every ten years, the U.S. Census Bureau counts the number of people who live in the United States, often including questions concerning age, race, relationships, gender, and income. Although the census is the Bureau's primary mission, it collects data on a wide range of categories throughout the year. The information is broken down into spatial areas called tracts, which allow data to be better understood as they apply to neighborhoods. Although communities often lack spatial limitations, there is a need to apply limitations when examining neighborhoods regarding race, income, and age.

3   Mixed-Income Neighborhoods in Chicago

Chicago was once known for its high-rise projects created by the Chicago Housing Authority (CHA). These projects quickly became synonymous with gang violence, poverty, and hopelessness in the United States. The condition of the CHA project deteriorated quickly after initial construction in 1942 until the final building was demolished in 2011. The planned mixed-income replacements for these projects are an attempt to advert the urban renewal that forced poor people into dislocated civilian status.

Beyond averting displacement of citizens, these new neighborhoods were created with the idea that fostering increased social capital and granting access to safer living conditions, better schools, and employment influence the lives of low-income residents positively. Destruction of old projects meant the CHA had to implement various methods of relocating residents, including forced relocation and use of housing vouchers. These acts resulted in many problems, from residents refusing to return to the new projects to the CHA losing residents in the system (Goetz, 2003; Smith et al., 2010). As residents returned to developments, neighborhoods divided between renters and owners and by socio-economic classes and races, while old prejudices crept into social interactions. Owners began to perceive all crimes were the product of living near poor youths, while renters began to resent rules put in place by homeowner associations. Public spaces became divided territories as disparate socio-economic groups laid claim to parks and streets (Chaskin & Joseph, 2009, 2011, 2012; Rosenbaum, Stroh, & Flynn 1998). Interactions among socio-economic groups, and among subgroups within socio-economic groups, were low (Rosenbaum et al., 1998).

Failing to ascertain the cultural differences and ensuring equal involvement of all parties in the creation and management of the neighborhood resulted in degradation of the unified community. However, poor planning for such an undertaking cannot be solely responsible for the situation (Joseph, 2010); failings inside the developments to integrate points to low resilience, and while it is easy to say low-income residents failed to acclimate to their new environment, neither side was able to acclimate to the mixed-income neighborhood.

PSOC, Cultural Citizenship and Positive Community Identity
Application of Brodsky et al.'s (1999) concept of PSOC to the Chicago neighborhoods indicates a low level of community, outside socio-economic groups. This finding demonstrates a need to identify the social issues that arise when mixing multiple socio-economic groups in common neighborhoods. On a smaller scale, Perkins (1982)

discovered that rallying an entrenched middle class to aid the poor results in rejection of social change. In these circumstances, it is important to implement community-driven planning (Jones, 1990). PSOC links deeply with cultural citizenship since an understanding of the system that is the community fosters positive outlooks toward community; cultural citizenship is not only the aversion of oppression, but also the understanding that one must work inside their own reality. These two, in turn, create a positive identity for the community.

4   YMCA Young Adult Services

Located in Seattle's Rainer Valley neighborhood, YMCA-YAS represents an interesting step in the process of becoming housed. Focusing on young adults aged 18 to 24, YMCA-YAS is a springboard for those looking to move beyond homelessness. It adheres to Hart's Ladder of Youth Participation (*what we're about: 2011-2012 priorities*, n.d.), working primarily with young adults who chose to become their own primary agents of housing (A. Fox, personal communication, January 23, 2013). In the view of YAS, these include those people who occupy the top three rungs of Hart's Ladder. Its residents emerge from three categories. First are homeless people living on the streets, couch surfers, and those lacking secure, permanent housing or shelter. Second are those at risk of homelessness, and third are foster children who have aged out of the system.

4.1   Structure of Young Adult Services

The YAS program of the YMCA is a continuum of services helping young adults work toward their goals of housing, employment, education, and life skills, while providing a safe environment for young adults to connect with peers and case managers, and relax and learn. The entire process is designed to move a client into employment, education, and permanent housing, and it starts when a client recognizes the need to move forward. Recognition derives from several places. For Sue, whose story is explored later, it started when she recognized that the situation in her parent's home was unstable and an occasionally abusive family environment. She had yet to acknowledge her status as at risk for homelessness, though she knew her housing situation was unstable at best. Her second recognition came after spending several months on a friend's couch. Although she understood her situation, it was through her social network at a community college that allowed her to seek housing. Sue, and others like her who recognize their situations and are ready to stabilize, are the young adults YAS serves.

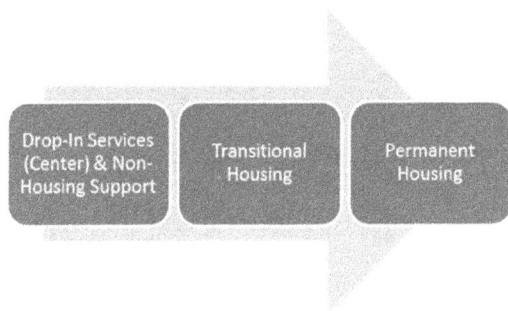

Figure 1: Resident's flow through the YAS branches.

Aaron Fox, a program manager for YAS, explained in an interview that YAS makes itself available to potential clients, then waits for them to apply through the Y's Center for Young Adults, or "The Center" (A. Fox, personal communication, January 23, 2013). The Center and The 2100 building that The Center occupies along with The Mockingbird Society and other foster care and youth outreach nonprofits offers a host of programs from college grants, jobs, internships, and volunteer opportunities to free lunches. A potential client needs only to talk with a staff member to find the right program. For those clients who wish to enter the transitional housing program, the application process involves three steps. Step 1 requires the applicant to attend a general orientation course that familiarizes him/her with the basic concepts and requirements of the YAS transitional housing program. This initial class does not require registration beyond becoming a Center member. Step 2 includes a series of three classes, for all of which the participant must register. The first class is an in-depth orientation on the transitional housing program. The second class covers financial management, and the third covers conflict resolution. In Step 3, the applicant schedules an interview with the program director. At this point, the applicant selects the house(s) that works best for him/her, and waits for his/her name to appear on the list (*Need Housing?*, n.d.).

At the time of the interview with Aaron Fox, the list had a back log of 30 clients waiting for openings in either one of the six shared homes or one of the 20 studio apartments in the Young Adults in Transition (YAIT) program. The program is geared toward young adults who aged out of foster care or those who are homeless. Once a client's name appears on the list, he/she interviews with the resident manager to ensure good fit with the house. Once in, the client has between 15 and 24 months of housing (depending on program) available (*get: [housing]*, n.d). In that time, the residents are supported by center staff members and a case manager to find work, obtain an education, and adjust to stable living.

4.2 Model of Involvement

The model of involvement and empowerment shown in Figure 2 shows a simplified version of a resident's path. Although the model appears as a circle, the goal is for a resident to move beyond transitional housing and into permanent housing, employment, financial security, and balanced health.

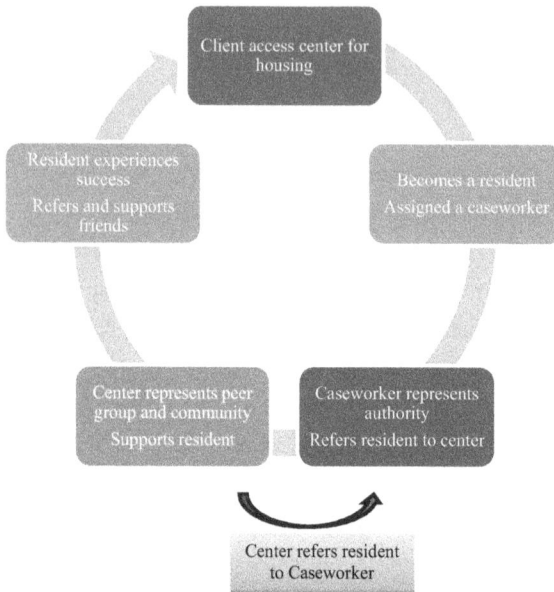

If a resident moves too quickly out of transitional housing and is not successful, he/she is usually welcomed back into the YAS transitional housing program.

The model does not fully illustrate a resident's commitment to the process. Each resident is required—in addition to paying rent—to commit to 30 hours of

Figure 2: YMCA Model of Involvement.

productivity a week. There is a slight difference between YAIT and shared home residents when it comes to what productivity represents. The difference is YAIT residents cannot be full-time students. Both YAIT residents and shared home residents must attend regular dinners (monthly for YAIT, weekly for houses), and complete 2 to 4 hours of volunteering each month. Beyond that, YAS is flexible concerning what constitutes productivity, and offers many opportunities for residents to complete requirements through YMCA programs such as WAGES, an 8-week paid internship that may become permanent employment, and volunteering at the center.

A house resident who is also full-time student may pay rent using student aid (though this is not considered the best solution), attend community college, a trade school, or university full-time, eat once a week with his/her housemates and resident manager, and volunteer at Lifelong AIDS Alliance for a few hours each month. The resident may also have a job, work at a non-profit such as The Mockingbird Society for a stipend, or any combination of career and life choices that work for him/her. Although residents are the primary agents, they work in partnership with YAS resource specialists (case managers) and resident managers. Resident managers represent stability and act in a parental or authoritative role. Meetings between residents and resident managers range from weekly to once a month (Pat[3], personal communication, March 7, 2013). Although a resident manager represents the parent, the relationship is cooperative, realizing the resident as a partner and participant, not a person directed and ordered through the process. This is better represented in the resident manager's secondary function of mentor. The resource specialists at YAS fill a different role, interacting at a peer level and acting as a sounding board and safety net for the residents. This relationship between staff members and residents exemplifies the role played by resource specialist Leon. Leon is a staff member at the YAS center. Eight years previously he was a resident in the YAS transitional housing program (Leon, personal communication, February 27, 2013). Moving from resident to employee, Leon experienced the mentoring relationship from both sides. Now specializing in education and employment resources, Leon views his role as a balance between peer and case manager. Operating in that gray area, Leon provides the positive knowledge and help residents such as Sue have come to expect from the Y (Sue[3], personal communication, February 11, 2013).

Aaron Fox attributes much of YAS's successes with clients to this model. The YAS program has few issues with violence, graffiti, or destruction of property from residents, and residents rarely become pregnant while living at the Y—all attributes that make the program unique nationally. This partnering model does not stop internally; it is practiced cross-institutionally since YAS works with YouthCare (WAGES is a YouthCare program), ROOTS young adult shelter, and many other organizations in the greater Seattle area.

Staff burnout. Burnout is common in many areas of society, both public and private, and the YMCA-YAS is no different in that regard. Burnout can reduce productivity in staff members so it is something to be avoided. The differences between burnout for an accountant, for example, and burnout for staff members at a resource center for homeless young adults are significant. Instead of numbers not adding up on a balance sheet, the lives of young men and women can be affected adversely—people who have already been through many negative experiences. To discourage burnout among staff members, YAS engages in counter-burnout measures. Staff members watch out for each other and engage in weekly and monthly meetings to discuss stress loads, projects, and burnout. YAS encourages healthy living, from eating fresh foods to eating away from your desk to upholding the idea that a healthy practitioner creates a healthy community. Although these measures are not a cure for burnout, the support system in place models the idea that communities aid the individual, and individual health is the health of the community. This is an important concept since it instills a village mentality that empowers the individual. This mentality is the same circular model that empowers the resident to work with a community on the journey to stabilization

ZIP Codes, Census Tracts & Housing Location

There are six shared homes and an apartment-based program (YAIT) in the YMCA-YAS program. Together, they represent housing for 48 young adults, 19 of which are studios in YAIT. With the exception of YAIT—which is located in the business district of downtown Seattle inside the YMCA—the houses are located in affluent neighborhoods (A. Fox, personal communication, January 23, 2013). Placement of the housing is important, influencing a sense of community held by residents. Therefore, income statuses for two of the houses—the West Seattle and Central Seattle houses—are examined using 2010 U.S. Census data. Tract data were drawn from the 2010 Census Interactive Population Search (n.d.) and the U.S. Census map King County (033) (*King County (033)* (205053033001), 2010). U.S. Census data at the ZIP Code level provided an overall view of the larger neighborhood.

West Seattle house, U.S. Census Tract no. 109, ZIP Code 98106.

Tract no. 109 has a population of 1287, of which 496 (39%) live in owner-occupied dwellings and 55% live in rented housing. One-thousand one-hundred twenty-four residents reported being 18 years or older, and the majority (703) were aged 25 to 49. Seventy percent self-reported as White[4] and 10% self-reported as Asian. African-American, American Indian and Alaskan Native, Native Hawaiian and Pacific Islander, and Other made up the remaining 20% (*2010 Census Interactive Population Search*, n.d.).

ZIP Code 98106 has a population of 22,873. The largest age group falls into the 25 to 49 range, comprising 35% of the population or 20% fewer than the 55% that comprised the same population in Tract no. 109 (*American factfinder – results*, n.d.a). The three largest sectors of employment for 98106 are (a) professional, scientific, management, administrative, and waste management services at 16.6%, (b) education services, healthcare, and social assistance at 18.2%, and (c) arts, entertainment, recreation, accommodation, and food services at 12%. Income for 98106 is concentrated in the $50,000 to $74,999 and $75,000 to $ 99,999 ranges, with 24.1% and 13.9%, respectively. The remainder of the population is concentrated below the $50,000 level, and 7.2% of the population reported earning fewer than $10,000 per annum (*American factfinder – results*, n.d.b). Education showed a spread that coincided with the employment sectors. For the 98106 ZIP Code, 26% of the population reported having some college, 21.9% reported a four-year degree, and 18% completed high school (excluding GEDs) (*American factfinder – results*, n.d.c). These data suggest a mixed-income and mixed-education population at the ZIP Code level.

Central house, U.S. Census Tract no. 76, ZIP Code 98112.

Tract no. 76 has a population of 3498, of which 1342 (39%) live in owner-occupied dwellings and 59% live in rented housing. Three-thousand eighty-six reported being 18 years or older, and the majority (2039) were aged 25 to 49. Seventy-six percent self-reported as White[4] and 11% self-reported as African American. Asian, American Indian and Alaskan Native, Native Hawaiian and Pacific Islander, and Other made up the remaining 13% (*2010 Census Interactive Population Search*, n.d.).

ZIP Code 98112 has a population of 21,077. The largest age groups fall into the 25 to 49 range, comprising 43% of the population or 15% fewer than the 58% that comprise the same population in Tract no. 76 (*American factfinder – results*, n.d.d). The two largest sectors of employment for 98112 are (a) professional, scientific, management, administrative, and waste management services at 24% and (b) education services, healthcare, and social assistance at 26.3%. Unlike 98106, no third sector employed more that 10% of the population. Income for 98112 showed a similar deviation from ZIP Code 98106. Income was concentrated at the $50,000 to $74,999, $100,000 to 149,999, and $200,000 and greater brackets, with 15%, 17%, and 17%, respectively (*American factfinder – results*, n.d.e). Education showed a spread that coincided with the employment sectors. For the 98106 ZIP Code, 37% of the population reported having a four year degree and 38% a graduate or professional degree. Only 12% reported having some college, but no degree, and 5.5% had a high school education (excluding GEDs) (*American factfinder – results*, n.d.f).

Unlike the West Seattle house, the Central house is located in a dual-income environment that favors the upper income brackets. This is also reflected in the levels of education, where 38% reported a post-graduate education. Unlike the West Seattle house, the Central house is not situation in a mixed-income neighborhood, but it is located in an upper-class area.

5.   Story of Sue[3]

Sue's story is both sad and triumphant. Sad because her situation is common among Americans, but triumphant because she moved beyond her initial environment and grew as a person and member of her community. Sue was an only child, and did not meet her biological father until she was in her late teens. In Sue's early years, she suffered poverty, kidnapping by a mentally ill friend of her mother, and a life where she and her mother were never far from homelessness. Later, her mother met and married her stepfather, the man she has since referred to as dad. As Sue grew up, her parents had two more children and moved many times following work and the hope of a stable life. Sue, quickly became a second mother to her siblings, further linking her to the family as a needed resource. Living in poverty, with working poor parents and two dependent siblings, Sue felt trapped. Eventually she escaped to Cascades Job Corps Center with a young man, her fiancé. The environment and isolation was no different for Sue, and the man she thought she would marry turned abusive; once again Sue was moving. Having completed her GED at Job Corps but not her job training, Sue was left unemployed and living between her parents' apartment and the family of her new boyfriend.

Sue felt something no middle-class American may truly understand: the knowledge that she must escape, but lacking the social and economic resources to do so. When Sue's father found work in a pie factory in Spokane, she readied herself for another move. Spokane was a different environment for Sue. Her family moved from the urban slums of Everett to a suburban neighborhood in southeast Spokane. Her father obtained stable work at a pie factory, and her siblings had a yard for the first time. For a short time, Sue held a job while exploring the tribulations of being a first-generation college student. Her family life, however, was unstable. She quickly fell into the role of homemaker and parent to her siblings while her father worked the third shift. Her parents fought and talked of divorce, and her father drank. She lost her job due to a misbalanced till, missed a quarter of school, and began to fall into the old habits of despair. Most of Sue's social capital was negative; her friends, family, and environment centered on a culture of poverty. Her father lost his job, her parents were fighting, and her mother was seeing another man. Their housing relied on her brother's disability check and the good graces of their landlord.

In November 2011, Sue went to Seattle to visit friends, one of many trips she took to keep a grip on her sanity as her life's dreams slipped away. During this trip, she found herself signed up by a friend for a new student open house at Seattle University and Seattle Central

Community College (SCCC). Suddenly things seemed brighter. At Seattle University, Sue discovered a world of education where she was more than a number, and she had her first positive experience with Christians. SCCC was equally refreshing; Sue remembers her excitement when the quarterly schedule at SCCC contained more classes than Spokane's yearly catalogue. A deal was struck quickly for temporary housing with friends for the Fall 2012 quarter, but Sue was still unsure. Her family needed her, her siblings depended on her, and what would happen if the divorce was finalized?

A month later, the deteriorating situation in Spokane forced her decision. Sue needed to leave soon. She called her friends in Seattle and reworked her plans so she could come at the end of winter quarter, two quarters earlier than before. Given these conditions, she enrolled at SCCC, with her FAFSA completed and school paid for. Her motivation was high, and she was on her way to Seattle by the end of winter quarter. Sue's life after the move was one of momentous change. Merely being in a positive environment improved her outlook on life. Although she spent several months sleeping on a friend's couch, engaged in a fruitless search for work, she enrolled at SCCC and joined the First Generation Students Club. At the same time, she was enjoying her volunteer time at Lifelong AIDS Alliance. Her social network was moving away from those trapped in poverty to those who saw poverty as a momentary setback on the road to a happier life. However, she was running out of time; she could not live on a couch forever. Again her new social network aided her. A friend and previous participant in the Y's YAIT program told her about The Center, and Sue reached a point where she could control her own life.

By February 2013, Sue had spent four months in the YAS transitional housing program. She has gotten to know her flat mates and neighborhood. Her neighbors however were quite a different story. Sue explains that the houses are quite nice, and the people are friendly, but she does not feel a part of the community. When asked whether she would attend community events, she stated she would not feel comfortable enough to attend. For Sue, this lack of community derived from the income gap between her and her neighbors, the number of young parents in the area, and a feeling that many of her neighbors had lived in the area for decades or generations (Sue[3], personal communication, February 2, 2013). She was the opposite. Coming from a family that battled poverty and moved frequently, Sue found little common ground with her neighbors, and her psychological sense of community was low.

However, her sense of community in the YAS program was the opposite, and Sue believed the program helped stabilize her and other participants. Sue felt she could relate to YAS staff members. To her, they represented a group of people just old enough to give advice, but young enough to understand where participants were coming from. The opposite sense of community existed there for her; instead of one with which she interacted politely, she had one with which she could engage actively. Although she had been involved with the program for only four months, Sue engaged with her peers as a volunteer at The Mockingbird Society and a young student at SCCC. Earlier skills of adaptability learned through her childhood were being put to use, helping others whose housing is at-risk, aiding first-generation college students, and spending time with her friend. The environment of support, healthy living, and caring created by YAS enabled this change. Sue made the decisions, Sue decided to change her life, and Sue created an example for her siblings to follow in subsequent years. Sue is why YAS looks for those young adults who are ready for change, and why its success rate is high.

6   Results

The maximum population for YAS transitional housing residents is 48, including the 19 studio apartments located at the downtown Seattle YMCA building (YAIT) and the six shared homes located in the greater Seattle area. Those houses are located in Bellevue, Central Seattle, North Seattle, Auburn, West Seattle, and Shoreline. Of the 29 residents located in residential neighborhoods, 21% (6) of the maximum population returned surveys, and 1 of the 20 maximum population from the YAIT program returned surveys. Of the seven surveys issued to resident managers, three were returned. Participation by resident managers did not predict participation by residents. For example, no resident manager returned a survey for YAIT or the Central house, but one resident from each returned a survey. Similarly, the Bellevue resident manager returned a survey, but none of the Bellevue Residents returned surveys.

Time was a factor of the ability to participate (M. Harvey, personal communication, February 18, 2013). Michele Harvey, resident manager of the West Seattle house, explained that the residents often have heavy or odd schedules due to work, volunteer time, and school (M. Harvey, personal communication, February 18, 2013). Of the three residents at the West Seattle house, one is finishing her degree, one is an AmeriCorps VISTA member, and the third is a full-time volunteer readying to transition out of housing. Respondents from the Shoreline and Central houses reported similar trends.

The issue of availability resurfaced during the interviews. Resident schedules often conflicted, making interviews with some such as those at the Bellevue house impossible. Regardless, some residents and resident managers attempted to arrange for alternate interview times. Lack of availability of residents meant clarifications to survey answers were not obtainable. For example, residents at the Shoreline house reported they did not feel comfortable in the community, but since they were unable to participate in the interview process and did not elaborate on the survey, it is unknown why these respondents felt this way.

Surveys

The surveys (Appendix I) captured two types of data, demographic and subjective. The demographic data were interpreted easily since respondents needed only to check boxes indicating age, marital status, gender, and education. The subjective data however represent respondents' general feelings, unless respondents chose to expand on their answers in the free-write section.

Demographics Answers. Seven residents responded to the survey. Of these seven, five identified their gender as women and two as men. No participant identified as transgendered. Four were single and three were with partners (i.e., a boyfriend or girlfriend). None reported as married. Status as partnered was not dependent on age, gender, or time in the program. Ages ranged from 18 to 24 years, with the majority of respondents reporting being between 21 and 23 years old. Two respondents had been in the program for a year or more. All had at least a high school education or equivalent, and many had some college education beyond that. One respondent reported having completed a four-year degree, and two respondents are expecting completion of their associate's degrees in the 2014 school year.

Subjective Answers. Three subjective questions centered on how respondents viewed and accessed their communities. These questions asked respondents about their feelings toward housemates and neighborhoods, and whether they used community resources (Appendix IV). Regarding spending time with housemates, residents preferred not to, opting either to spend time alone or with others outside the house. However, residents did not indicate they disliked their housemates; the simply preferred to spend time with others.

Regarding feelings concerning neighborhoods, two respondents felt a part of their neighborhood, while the other five reported they merely lived in the neighborhood and either felt uncomfortable around neighbors or spent time outside their neighborhood. Finally, respondents reported they use community spaces; five of seven reported they used libraries, parks, civic buildings, and community centers.

Interviews

Five residents were available for interviews. Of these residents, one was from YAIT, one from Central house, and three from West Seattle house. Four were women and one was a man. Regardless of house or gender, interviewees expressed an understanding of the YAS program, its requirements, and resources available to them. The residents referred to the community presented by the center in a more positive light than the spatial community in which they lived. All expressed long-term goals on which they were currently working. For example, Tom[3] reported a desire for financial stability and obtaining checking and savings accounts (Tom, personal communication, February 27, 2013). Dina[3] was completing her cosmetology degree, specializing in hair (Dina, personal communication, March 7, 2013), and Sue[3] was exploring schools at which to complete her four-year degree (Sue, personal communication, February 5, 2013). West Seattle house residents expressed a sense of safety and a high level of comfort in their neighborhood. Dina[3] and Pat[3] stated neighbors were polite and warm, though they did not interact with them directly (Dina and Pat, personal communication, March 7, 2013). When asked whether they would attend a community event such as a block party, all three responded they would.

Sue[3] felt at odds with her neighborhood. Although she felt safe and welcome, the socio-economic status of the Central house's neighborhood was apparent to her, and she did not feel comfortable participating in community events (Sue, personal communication, February 11, 2013). Tom,[3] a resident from YAIT, was an anomaly among the other participants. Living in downtown Seattle does not offer people the same opportunities to interact with a neighborhood. However, he believed strongly that YMCA staff members provided a sense of community, one that supported him and his fellow residents. Staff members represented positive social capital, which afforded access to jobs and subsequent housing opportunities that were unobtainable through peer groups (Tom, personal communication, February 22, 2013).

7 Conclusions

As a population, residents of the YMCA-YAS transitional housing programs appear to have a sense of community connected to both YMCA staff members and outside peer groups. Housing locations themselves do not appear to contribute to a sense of community, but this does not mean housing placement negates community. In interviews, one of the most important parts of the housing program was the sense of safety felt within neighborhoods. Safety influenced the residents' abilities to form new communities positively, granting them a sense of stability and empowering them to pursue goals without added stress of being mugged, assaulted, or exposed to gang violence, events common in low-income neighborhoods. Placement of housing in safe, affluent, or mixed-income neighborhoods means success. Residents expressed a sense of cultural citizenship. In both interviews and surveys, participants reported an understanding of the power afforded them through the YAS program and their options inside their socio-economic classes. Coupled with feelings of community toward the YMCA-YAS programs and positive resilience demonstrated by entering the program, psychosocial sense of community was high among residents.

8 Recommendations

Mentioned in the limitations section, this study cannot be generalized beyond the respondents who participated in this study. To do so, this study would need to expand longitudinally, following several residents though their journeys with the YMCA-YAS, with standardized entry, exit, and update surveys collected at various periods. A study of that magnitude would be useful to examine the true sense of community found in the program. Were a study to include housing similar to YouthCare, more would be revealed concerning how housing from various organizations influences residents. The work performed by YMCA-YAS staff members has been essential to the success of the program. Staff members are active, open, and involved at a level that invites even those turned off by social services to return to the profession (Leon, personal communication, February 22, 2013). I recommend YMCA-YAS staff members sustain current levels of excellence in providing safe and positive environments where participants and residents can springboard from homelessness to bring housed.

9   References

2010 Census Interactive Population Search. (n.d.). `Retrieved from http://www.census.gov/2010census/popmap/ipmtext.php?fl=53:53033http

American factfinder - results. (n.d.a). Retrieved from

http://factfinder2.census.gov/faces/tableservices/jsf/pages/productview.xhtml?pid=DEC_10_
    DP_DPDP1

American   factfinder   -   results.   (n.d.b).   Retrieved   from
    http://factfinder2.census.gov/faces/tableservices/jsf/pages/productview.xhtml?pid=AC
    S_11_5YR_DP03

American factfinder - results. (n.d.c). Retrieved from

http://factfinder2.census.gov/faces/tableservices/jsf/pages/productview.xhtml?pid=ACS_11_
    5YR_DP02

American   factfinder   -   results.   (n.d.d).   Retrieved   from
    http://factfinder2.census.gov/faces/tableservices/jsf/pages/productview.xhtml?pid=DE
    C_10_DP_DPDP1

American   factfinder   -   results.   (n.d.e).   Retrieved   from
    http://factfinder2.census.gov/faces/tableservices/jsf/pages/productview.xhtml?pid=AC
    S_11_5YR_DP03

American   factfinder   -   results.   (n.d.f).   Retrieved   from
    http://factfinder2.census.gov/faces/tableservices/jsf/pages/productview.xhtml?pid=AC
    S_11_5YR_DP02

Boff, L. (1997). *Cry of the earth, cry of the poor.* Maryknoll, NY: Orbis Press.

Brodsky, A. E., O'Campo, P. J., & Aronson, R. E. (1999). PSOC in community context:
    Multi-level correlates of a measure of psychological sense of community in low-
    income, urban neighborhoods. *Journal of Community Psychology, 27*(6), 659-679.

Chaskin, R. J. (2008). Resilience, community, and resilient communities: Conditioning contexts and collective action. *Child Care in Practice, 14*(1), 65-74. doi:10.1080/13575270701733724

Chaskin, R. J., & Joseph, M. L. (2009). Building "community" in mixed-income developments: Assumptions, approaches and early experiences. *Urban Affairs Review, 45*(3), 299-335. doi:10.1177/1078087409341544

Chaskin, R. J., & Joseph, M. L. (2011). Social interaction in mixed-income developments: relational expectations and emerging reality. *Journal of Urban Affairs, 33*(2), 209-237. doi:10.1111/j.1467-9906.2010.00537.x

Chaskin, R. J., & Joseph, M. L. (2012). 'Positive' gentrification, social control and the 'right to the city' in mixed-income communities: Uses and expectations of space and place. *International Journal of Urban and Regional Research, 37*(5), 1-23. doi:10.1111/j.1468-2427.2012.01158.x

Chaskin, R. J., & Karlström, M. (2012). *Beyond the neighborhood: Policy engagement and systems change in the new communities program.* Retrieved from http://www.mdrc.org

Claridge, T. (2012). *Definitions of social capital.* Retrieved from http://www.socialcapitalresearch.com/definition.html

Count us in: King Country's point-in-time count of homeless & unstably house young people. Retrieved from http://www.youthcare.org/sites/default/files/Final%20Count%20Us%20In%20Report%202013.pdf

Edles, L. D., & Appelrouth, S. (2010). *Sociological theory in the classical era.* Thousand Oaks, CA: Pine Forge Press.

Felt, C. (2011). *King County experiences strong population growth according to 2010 census results.* Retrieved from http://www.kingcounty.gov/exec/news/release/2011/February/24Census.aspx

Galster, G., & Zobel, A. (1998). Will dispersed housing programmes reduce social problems in the US? *Housing Studies, 13*(5), 605-622.

get: [housing]. (n.d.). Retrieved from http://www.ymcayas.org/what-were-about/2894.aspx

Goetz, E. G. (2003). Housing dispersal programs. *Journal of Planning Literature, 18*(1), 3-16.

Groody, D. (2009). *Globalization, spirituality, and justice*. Maryknoll, NY: Orbis Books.

Jackson, K. (1985). *Crabgrass frontier: The suburbanization of the United States*. New York, NY: Oxford University Press.

Jones, B. (1990). *Neighborhood planning: A guide for citizens and planners*. Chicago, IL: American Planning Association.

Jospeh, M. (2010). Creating mixed-income developments in Chicago: Developer and service provider perspectives. *Housing Policy Debate*, 20(1), 91-118. doi:10.1080/10511481003599894

Kang, H. (2010). *Cultural citizenship and immigrant community identity: Constructing a multi-ethnic Asian American community*. El Paso, TX: LFB Scholarly Publishing.

Karlan, D., & Appel, J. (2011). *More than good intentions: How new economics is helping solve global poverty*. New York, NY: Penguin Group.

Katz, C., Liebow, E., & O'Malley, G. (2006). Building community during HOPE VI redevelopment: Lessons from a Seattle case study. *Human Organization, 62*(2), 192-202. doi:0018-7259/06/020192-11$1.60/1 /

King County (033) (205053033001). (2010, December 12). Retrieved from http://www2.census.gov/geo/maps/dc10map/tract/st53_wa/c53033_king/DC10CT_C5 3033_001.pdf

Martin, M. E. (2011). *Introduction to human services: Through the eyes of practice settings* (2nd ed.). Boston, MA: Allyn & Bacon.

Murrin, J. M., Johnson, P. E., McPherson, J. M., Gerstle, G., Rosenberg, E. S., & Rosenberg, N. L. (2008). *Liberty, equality, power: Volume II: Since 1863* (4th ed.). Belmont, CA: Thomson Higher Education.

Naveh, E. J. (1992). *Crown of thorns: Political martyrdom in America from Abraham Lincoln to Martin Luther King, Jr.* New York, NY: NYU Press

Need Housing?. (n.d.) Seattle WA: The YMCA

Perkins, J. (2007). *With justices for all: A strategy for community development* (3rd ed).Ventura, CA: Regal

Resistance. (2013). In *Oxford Dictionary*. Retrieved from http://oxforddictionaries.com/definition/english/resistance

Rosenbaum, J. E., Stroh, L. K., & Flynn, C. A. (1998). Lake Parc Place: A study of mixed-income housing. *Housing Policy Debate, 9*(4), 703-740.

Sampson, R. J. (1999). What community supplies. In R. F. Ferguson & W. T. Dickens (Eds.), *Urban problems and community development* (pp. 241-292). Washington D.C.: The Brookings Institution.

Schill, M. H. (Ed.). (1999). *Housing and community development in New York City: Facing the future*. Albany, NY: State University of New York Press.

Smith, R., Kingsley, G. T., Popkin, S., Dumlao, K., Ingrid, G. E., Joseph, M., & McKoy, D. (2010). Monitoring success in choice neighborhoods: A proposed approach to performance measurement. Retrieved from http://www.urban.org/

Stoutland, S. E. (1999). Community development corporations: Mission, strategy, and accomplishments. In R. F. Ferguson & W. T. Dickens (Eds.), *Urban problems and community development* (pp. 193-240). Washington D.C.: The Brookings Institution.

Vissing, Y. M. (1996). *Out of sight, out of mind: Homeless children and families in small-town America*. Lexington, KY: University Press of Kentucky.

what we're about: 2011-2012 priorities. (n.d.). Retrieved from http://www.ymcayas.org/what-were-about/2894.aspx

White. (n.d.). Retrieved from http://factfinder2.census.gov/help/en/glossary/w/white.htm

Why are youth homeless? (n.d.). Retrieved from http://www.youthcare.org/our-approach/why-are-youth-homeless

Wier, M. (1999). Power, money and politics in community development. In R. F. Ferguson & W. T. Dickens (Eds.), *Urban problems and community development* (pp. 139-192). Washington D.C.: The Brookings Institution.

Wilma, D. (2001). Seattle neighborhoods: Revenna – Roosevelt – thumbnail history. Retrieved from http://www.historylink.org/index.cfm?DisplayPage=output.cfm&File_Id=3502

10   Appendix I

Young Adult Resident Survey

Thank you for taking the time to fill out this survey. It is my hope that this survey will help designers of future short term programs to meet the needs of residents. At the end of this survey please feel free to add any comments or suggestions that you may have to improve your particular program. Your answers will be kept confidential (no names are to be used on this survey).

Again thank you for your time and your participation.

Name of House: _____

Gender: ☐Woman ☐Man ☐Transgendered ☐Other_____

Marital Status: ☐Married ☐Partnered (Have a boyfriend or girlfriend) ☐Single

Parental Status: ☐No children ☐Have children not living with me

Age:☐18 ☐19 ☐20 ☐21 ☐22 ☐23 ☐24

How many months have you lived in the house: _____

Occupation (Check all that apply):
☐ Employed ☐Volunteer ☐Student

	Hours / Credits Per Week						
Employed	☐0-3hr	☐4-6hr	☐7-9hr	☐10-12hr	☐13-15hr	☐ 15-18	☐ 19+hr

Volunteer	☐0-9hr	☐10-14hr	☐15-19	☐20-24	☐25-29	☐30-35	☐36-40
Student	☐ Not Enrolled	☐¼ Time	☐½ Time	☐¾ Time	☐ Full Time		

Highest Level of Education (If in progress please include expectant date of completion):

☐High School / GED: _____

☐Vocational Training: Major: _____

☐Associates Degree: Major: _____

☐Technical Degree: Major: _____

☐Bachelor's Degree: Major: _____

Community:

This section examines your feeling of community and involvement, both in your housing and in your local community.

- **How do you feel about your housemates?**

    ☐I enjoy interacting with my housemates and do so often.

    ☐I enjoy interacting with my housemates, but prefer to spend my free time alone.

    ☐I prefer to spend my free time with friends who live outside of my house

    ☐I only live at the house; I do not like interacting with others outside group events.

- **How do you feel about your Neighborhood?**

    ☐I feel like I am part of the neighborhood and feel comfortable around my neighbors.

    ☐I feel like I am part of the neighborhood, but sometimes feel uncomfortable around my neighbors.

    ☐I do not feel like I am part of my neighborhood, I feel uncomfortable around my neighbors.

    ☐I just live in the house; I spend most of my time outside the neighborhood.

- Do you use common community spaces, such as parks, libraries, civic buildings and community centers?

  ☐Yes ☐ No

- I use the following common community spaces:

  ☐Parks ☐Libraries ☐Civic Buildings ☐Community Centers

- If you use community spaces please list activities. Include taking classes, hanging out with friends, reading, relaxing or any other activity.

  _____

  _____

  _____

  _____

  _____

- Please list the services and programs provided by YMCA in which you are a participating in. If you participate in YouthCare programs that are offered through YMCA, please list those as well with an "YC" next to it.

  _____

  _____

  _____

  _____

  _____

- Please take this space to share your goals and or suggestions for your program. Please feel free to continue onto the back pages.

  _____

  _____

  _____

  _____

  _____

  _____

  _____

- **Please take this space to share your goals and or suggestions for your program. Please feel free to continue onto the back pages.**

  _____

  _____

  _____

11 Appendix II

Resident Manager Email Interview Questions

Thank you for taking the time to be part of this interview. These questions are a transcript of the questions that will be asked to those participating in the phone interviews, for those who complete these questions, but would still like to conduct a phone interview, our discussions will center on your answers and questions you may have about the study.

Once the form is completed please return it (in paper or electronic form) to either Aaron Fox or myself at the provided addresses. Please feel free to contact me via email if you have any questions, comments or suggestions.

Geri Madsen
324 Summit Ave E
Seattle WA 98102
gerald.madsen@hotmail.com

Aaron Fox
afox@seattleymca.org

*Name:_____   *Age:_____

House:_____   *Gender:_____

*Optional

1) What interested you in becoming a Resident Manager for YMCA YAS?

2) How long have your worked as a Resident Manager for YMCA YAS, and have you been a resident manager before?

3) How do you see your role in the house? Is it one of mentor, mediator, a person who provides a stable and supportive environment or a mix of different roles?

4) In your opinion, what do you think of the neighborhood surrounding your house? Do you feel they are supportive of the house?

5) In your opinion, do your residents think of the house as a community or family?

6) As a resident manager, how would you like to see the program progress from here?

12 Appendix III

Resident Survey List

Resident List n=6							
Participant	Pseudo-Name	Resident Status	Age	Residency (Months)	Gender	House	Interview
Participant 1	Sue	Current	21	4	Woman	Central	Y
Participant 2	Sarah	Current	23	UNK	Woman	WSH*	Y
Participant 3	Ralph	Current	23	4	Man	Shoreline	N
Participant 4	Emily	Current	18	6.5	Woman	Shoreline	N
Participant 5	Pat	Current	21	24	Woman	WSH*	N
Participant 6	Dina	Current	21	15	Woman	WSH*	N
Participant 7	Tom	Current	20	5	Man	YAIT	Y

*West Seattle House

13   Appendix IV

Answers to Resident Survey Subjective Questions

How do you feel about your house mates:

I enjoy interacting with my housemates and do so often.	3
I enjoy interacting with my housemates, but prefer to spend my free time alone.	2
I prefer to spend my free time with friends who live outside of my house	2
I only live at the house; I do not like interacting with others outside group events.	

How do you feel about your Neighborhood?

I feel like I am part of the neighborhood and feel comfortable around my neighbors.	2
I feel like I am part of the neighborhood, but sometimes feel uncomfortable around my neighbors.	
I do not feel like I am part of my neighborhood, I feel uncomfortable around my neighbors.	2
I just live in the house; I spend most of my time outside the neighborhood.	3

Do you use common community spaces, such as parks, libraries, civic buildings and community centers?

Yes	5
No	2

14   Endnotes

1. Since Perkins believes his actions are a result of a calling from God, not a secular responsibility as seen in non-religious practitioners, I labeled his actions as Christian instead of those of a development practitioner. He might disagree since he describes what he does as urban community development.

2. For example: section 8 housing certificates, staggered rates and below-market rent, VA mortgage certificates for military veterans, and interest subsidies in the form of tax relief for mortgage dwellings.

3. Participants' names were changed for anonymity. To improve exposition of the findings, false names were given to each respondent. Refer to Appendix III for participant numbers that correspond with each pseudonym.

4. For 2010, the U.S. Census Bureau defined White as "A person having origins in any of the original peoples of Europe, the Middle East, or North Africa" (*White*, n.d.). This includes people with ethnic backgrounds of Hispanic, Arabic, Irish, Anglo-Saxon, Germanic, Egyptian, etc.

www.ingramcontent.com/pod-product-compliance
Lightning Source LLC
Chambersburg PA
CBHW032044040426
42334CB00038B/702